To: Love
From: Son Muya

DREAMS

The Classic Edition

SPONSORSHIP PAGE

Dreams ExCorporated Publishing
Proudly Presents:

DREAMS

The Classic Edition

Narrated By:

ARIEL MUYA

DREAMS
By Ariel Muya
Copyright: Ariel Muya 2020
ISBN: 978-0-692-87638-1
Published by Dreams ExCorporated
From The East Side with Love
All Rights Reserved
The Classic Edition

The Classic Edition

DREAMS

The Classic Edition

A Poem of Love

They say Love is the cure
So, I hope yours is so pure
That it'll make all the worlds pain disappear
And it makes up for all the tears we've endured
This is to the ones with Dreams uninsured
Blessings are here! We got our names secured.
If the present is a gift, then know that Love is here

DREAMS

The Classic Edition

Contents

(Guidelines to Get Off the Sidelines)

DREAMS

The Classic Edition

DREAMS

The Classic Edition

THE FOREWARD

Can't front, not long ago I wanted to die
Now the way my smile shines
It'll make you say How Sway!
To the first line
It's amazing how life changes
You're sinking one moment
Then suddenly, you're rising the next!
Can't front these lyrics I too didn't expect
But I'm thankful for its extract
Cause I think I made it!
I see Love all around me
Got the whole fam with me
Sorry to make it all about me
But I finally Love Me!
See Self-Love is the best drug
Took twenty-five years
But jokes on you we still alive!
Now go ahead and throw your hands up in the sky!
It's time to toast to our arise!

DREAMS

The Classic Edition

DREAMS

The Classic Edition

ACT 1:

THE RISE

OF THE

DREAMERS

DREAMS

The Classic Edition

A Poem of Dreams

Papa, what's a Dream?

Anything that you desire my Son.

Anything in the whole wide world Papa?

Yes, anything that your light touches.

What light of mine, Papa?

The one in your Heart, my Son.

DREAMS

This is Malcolm X redeemed

America's worst nightmare

Please tell me how does it feel?

I'm something like Achilles without the heel

So like Troy, I lay siege whenever these words spill

See each word is like a bullet

Making every line a loaded clip

Meaning every verse is a hearse

Sleep on me, you'll meet the cousin of her

Not placing these words as a curse

But rather the cure.

Loves Review (Still We Rise)

Trying to give the world my Dreams of Freedom

By painting out with these words how my soul sings

So, know each letter you read…

Is just a teardrop dripping from my Heart!

Went through school being told I'd be another statistic

I swear the system is sadistic, real imperialistic

Swear they even try to make us hate reading by
assigning us four-page reviews

Hey teacher, can I instead write what I see on the news?

They canceling all the programs for after school

Mamas always work doubles, so who makes our rules?

That's why we never think twice before we hit snooze

Not finger-pointing, I know teachers are underpaid too

I just want to know why when I turn on the news

I see things that only make me feel blue?

I thought the youth was the future

But our rulers seem to only view us as tumors

I mean introduce us to trappers before leaders

Ever wonder how we become pushers and shooters?

Don't take no doctorate to know

How Love should be tutored…

The Classic Edition

The Lost Boys (Ghetto Dreams)

When did suburban kids start having ghetto dreams?

Do they not know the horrors that the ghetto brings?

Have they never heard the sounds of a mother's screams?
(that's the sirens from the ambulance's coming up the street)

Have they never seen the sight of a mother's tears?
(that's the blood from her child flowing down the street)

Really when did suburban kids start having ghetto dreams?

I guess captain hook finally got his hook on them too

I hear songs of lost boys off loud falling from the moon

I hear songs of lost boys off lean sinking to the ground

I hear songs of lost boys off goose drowning in a pool

First Flight (The New Peter Pan)

I remember the midnight that my cousin first
passed me some loud

He told me' Keep it down…

And, made me promise to be careful if I ever soar and
he's not around

I was only 14 when I first danced on some clouds

Now in no way am I cursing him for putting me on

He only saw the stress in my eyes

That came from living so long

So, like a Doctor, he prescribed to me a realm

That'll forever make me feel young.

The Classic Edition

The Projects

The war on drugs was our dismay

1964 we got our civil rights

How else could life get this way?

Name other reasons that our babies are getting hit by strays?

I know we're scared but let us just refollow the trail

Cause will see the betrayal for the paper trail

I heard the first pushers were government agents in flashy cars

See, they studied us and the result

They sought we wanted to live life like flashy stars

That's why old heads called it the projects

That's why chuck berry was a rock star

Please take a moment to ask yourself

What songs did we use to sing before we were trap stars?

Here is a clue, Harriet Tubman was a conductor

Strange Plants

Ghetto streets bear a strange plant

Blood on the petals and blood on its stems

Black bodies lying all over ghetto corners

Strange plants sprouting

All because they're affiliated to different streets corners

Nightmarish scenes of a rebellious ghetto

Picture a sunny summer day with no clouds on the way

And all the kids from the block are outside at play

The echoes from their laughter

Swear it's so soulfully soothing

Then like lightning striking the sky

It flashes to a reign of shouts of terror

Another shot down by a stray.

Here are plants to add to the statistics

Here are plants to which's pain we reap forever

Here are plants for mamas to water with tears gushing from their eyes

Here comes summer…

The start of a strange and bitter harvest

The Classic Edition

A Letter From The Go

What options do we have concerning where we're from? Have you ever thought it might have something to do with the way that we live? So, can you shun me for my means if it's meant to be justified by my ends? Please don't preach to me about God because we know him, too, where I'm from. So, if Jesus ate with tax collectors and prostitutes, then He is riding with the pushers too through the mean windy city streets where bangers don't care who they shoot.

If trapping paid for these brand-new J's and schools won't pay for brand news hoops, I guess that makes it when it comes down to street smarts or book smarts it's not really that hard to choose. Especially when only one option seems to get you loot. I don't care if these words earn your boos, but blacks haven't really been given all their dues. That's the pun to the joke of why we act like we don't got all our screws. But then again, you'll never accept my view, so I'll just continue to sing my blues and sip my brews, all I'm saying is' How you going to shun me for a life I didn't choose?

- A Scared Child

27

Reality

They say in life you make your own bed

So, am I wrong to ask how we're born to ghetto streets?

I know our ancestors sewed the slave master's sheets

With Dreams that one day that their seeds will succeed

But the media keeps telling me

It won't be a reality

Unless we secede

At least that's the message I receive

When they kill us each week!

But hypocrisy from our own is the last thing we need

Cause blacks kill blacks every day

But that message is almost never perceived

Please don't misquote my allegiances is to Unity

But since the media isn't giving us anything to redeem

Tell me in what should I believe?

The Classic Edition

Over North

Don't pull my card, Sisters. I'm not banging.

I'm from the Cities where the worst fear is getting lost

Like responding to text messages'

Party over north where you at?

Can you blame us?

We were suburban kids just trying to be ahead of the herd

Pick up a few new terms

So, the Camille's of the world wouldn't look at me as a nerd.

Why do some girls prefer bad boys with hood demeanors?

I'm not hating just asking about the world we live in

Now from the burbs to the hood, we're all sleazing

Living fast till the day we die young

Cause that's the motto at devil's point

That's the night someone asks' Homie where you from?

This Psalm is dedicated to all the mamas crying at their child's face pastured on the morning news.

BLACK NEWS

Why when I turn on the local news and see black people

All I ever really see is sad people?

The trip though

Most the time they're usually talking about dead people

People dead by the hands of their people

I wonder who gave us the guns to kill our people?

I wonder who gave us the drugs to sell to our people?

I wonder who made it unsafe for black people to live
around black people?

The news anchor tells me it's black people

But hey Mr. news anchor, can I ask one question?

How did we go from Civil Rights to the war on drugs?

He responds' That's all the time that we have for tonight

Stay tuned Black-ish is on next!

The Classic Edition

Me Against The World (Do For Love)

With all this extra stressing

The question I wonder is after death, after my last breath

When will I finally get to rest through this oppression

My skin black so my self-defense is seen as aggression

Since King died my people haven't seen no progression

But then again who am I addressing

I'm lost I don't even know my own message

Won't even pray for blessings cause pain is its lesson

And God won't answer whenever I ask Him to lessen

Please don't miss quote whenever I question

Martyrdom

They Killed MLK

When he started the poor people's movement

That's poor blacks and whites working as one unit

They killed Malcolm X

When he stopped calling all white people devils

His eyes were opened to a world where all people could live as equals

They Killed Nat Turner

When he started a revolution

He saw slavery wasn't our revelation

The Classic Edition

Suicidal Mentality (Sing About Me)

When I die, who will sing about me?

At my funeral, I wonder what they'll say about me

Will I be nailed as a hero? Or praised as a foe?

Will they reminisce on all I stood for?

That's Love, just in case you didn't know.

When I die, will I have reached all my goals?

Or will I be a boy who strived to reach gold?

Worst fear is falling short

But I guess only time will tell

I read once that everything under the sun repeats itself

But has my tale really been told before?

Cause I want to be the Greatest Person ever to walk this earth

I want when anybody is in my presence, they never frown!

And, when anyone hears of my story

It makes them believe that they, too, can fly!

I want to show the whole world that when you dig deep

You can touch the sky!

But not going to lie

Most of the time all I can see is gray clouds in my sights

So, I get lost looking for Light

Forgetting the switch is my Heart

Neverland (Functioning Substance Abuser)

There was a time once when I never wanted to grow up

See I would fly through Neverland

And never want to land

I used to thank my imagination

Whenever it got me to this distant land

The pixie dust is what would have me zoning off on this trance

I would dance with my shadow as if we were listening to Dixieland

So, one day I proclaimed'

Surly this land must be heaven-sent

But as the words left my lips

Tinker bell glared at me with cold contempt

Then she flew to my shoulder and whispered in my ear'

No this isn't the promise land

Look to your feet you're sinking in quicksand.

The Classic Edition

The Chase

If thou hast run with the footmen

And they have wearied thee

Then how can thou contend with horses?

Run lost boy run captain hook is coming to get you

I said run lost boy run the world is trying to trap you

I heard Love is the only thing that can save you

I said fly lost child fly Heaven is above you

Temptations

Growing up

Thought kids could only get hooked on phonics

It's funny how life plays out

Guess Darren the lion couldn't save us all

A lost boy just hit my line up and said'

He got the plug on some chronic

A lost girl just sent me a snap asking'

Want to chill and fill our livers up with some toxins?

I'm kind of nauseous

Been trying to focus on the Dreams of Moses

But options be having me running away like Jonas.

The Classic Edition

Troubles

Woke up this morning hoping for a brighter day

See lately my clouds have been gray

I can't front though

Its cause my minds been swayed

By the finer things in life like'

What are we on today?

I could easily say peer pressure is to blame

But when the pressure busts

We'll all get drowned in the flood

Me Against The World Part 2 (If I Die Tonight)

I've been crying all morning, because of the nightmare I had last night. See, I was walking along the Jericho road, leaving my home behind me. The influences of life caused me to seek worldly pleasures.

My excuse is I couldn't handle the pressures to what I would be measured. Never did I like to heed to my Fathers lessons

But back to the passage of my journey through the barren desert. On a quest for worldly treasures but just right before Zion was out of my vision

I began second-guessing, wrestling in my head where am I headed? My dreams, have I forgotten?! Surely, I must turn back before my Love I forfeit!

But like a flash of lighting, A group of bandits appeared in the distance, and as our paths neared, one called to me asking' Boy, where are you headed? I told him' I'm going back home...

Swear those words never sounded so refreshing. But at my response, he glared cold contempt into my eyes, followed by an order to the others to rob me but keep me alive.

So, on Jericho's road there I laid

Alone, naked, beaten, barely breathing

Left to curse why I was still breathing

The Classic Edition

Runaways

They say we're lost, but really, we're just scared

Scared to leave Neverland because we might fall

Can you blame us for wanting to be alone in our own world?

At least here we're free to fly where ever we want to go

But to be honest, Love is what we're really trying to find

It's just we never found it in this here "free world"

We want to keep on fighting, but we only keep on dying

So, we keep on trying because it keeps us flying

I would say we're not addicted, but I'd only be lying

See we're all just scared to die

Because we don't know where our Hearts reside.

The Lost Boys Part 2 (Beautiful Nightmares)

Make way for a young Brother trying to make it

Field slave so best believe I'm going to take it

Real recognize real I'll die before I fake it

Had Dreams to be the world's greatest

But a black man with ambition

Learned the hard way the world hates it

Tried to find a prophet to tell me what my fate is

Money, Cash, and, Hoes the bill stated

We're all doomed if you needed that last line translated

But my minds so gated so I guess I could be mistaken

Either way for our ends we're all still waiting

The Classic Edition

For Whom The Bell Tolls (The Fall)

Used to say good things come to those that wait

But then I grew hungry staring at an empty plate

The message of this story is, what is Love for you to take?

My mistake is that I lust the stakes

Addicted so I can't find the breaks

Been mixing drinks to fight the pain

I can't take the ache

I'm on the edge of the ledge

Weak to some I know I seem

But I'm fighting voices in my head

Tempting me to make that last step

Me Against The World Part 3 (It Ain't Easy)

Suicidal mentality

Just don't got the heart for it

I'm not worried about what they'll say of me

More so, how my little sister will deal with it

So, for now, it's no belt when I take my car off parked

See I'm just trying to fast forward to the part I depart

And I don't even care if God sends me somewhere dark

Was it not His will for my Heart to come apart?

My life to come undone?

They're telling me repent

But when I awake the pain just restarts

The Classic Edition

Summer Dreams

If I could have one wish for summers

I would wish Brothers wouldn't kill one another

Then we could all catch fireworks instead of getting caught in fireworks during summers

I'm saying imagine no more ducking for cover

Imagine mothers not having to worry about our whereabouts when we're running late for supper

Imagine all smiles when we see each other

The prophecy is awesome a summer where no one suffers

Crazy it can all be achieved

If only we all believed.

DREAMS

The Classic Edition

ACT 2:

A

TALE

OF

TWIN CITIES

DREAMS

The Classic Edition

In this world, we get so lost with class, race, gender, age, and other things that we may think exalts us from the general population that we forget what unites us as one. Injustice anywhere is a threat to justice everywhere, so do on to others as you would like them to do on to you. I feel Freedom is so close, won't you lend me your hand so that we may reach it? If Jericho's wall fell, then the walls that separate us from being one will fall as well.

DREAMS

The Classic Edition

Cold World

Do you have some spare change?

The homeless shelter is full tonight

It's supposed to be ten below by nine, and I need money to rent a room so that I can survive the night

My heart stopped, and I muttered' Sorry man I don't have anything on me, and I don't have my card, so I can't get anything off me

To my response, he sighs

But before leaving my presence

He says to me'

God bless you.

In severe shock, I didn't know how to reply

Why would he ask Him to bless me

When to his needs, I can't even oblige?

So, without pride, I replied' God, bless you too

Twin City Blues

They say we're Minnesota nice

But I think some of us are just one step away

From slipping on thin ice

The motto here is'

Life can miss you if you blink twice!

So, the motivation is to get it

Even if it cost us our third strike.

Midwestern Dreamers aKa Loves Believers

If you want to reach us

Then tell us what Justin Henry's songs are about!

The Classic Edition

Moore Lake Drive

I know it's hard to have hope when you're broke

I remember Christmas's

Where my mom would quote' I'm broke

Swear that line always made my heart choke

Then only a week later I'd have to listen to other kids talk about their new toys

But see oddly from that pain a rose grew

And its loose screws gave it a world view

Mama dry your eyes

I'm humbled by all we've been through

Look at the Joy your Heart drew

Last Winter

His head collides with the hardwood floor

The collision detaches the note

Taped to the dark wood door

It floats down to where his bloodstream flows

It drowns slowly like a burning rose

Now the world will never know

The pain to which he wore

The pain is unbearable to both his folks

Because their son's pain was so unknown

Their teardrops keep the pain afloat

(Break)

I'm from the burbs where suicides aren't a joke

Learned the hard way

You don't have to be broke to lose control

So please always remember to bring hope to troubles door

Either by proofreading every note

Or being conscious of every joke

Because not doing either or

Maybe the cause of a mother's stroke.

Angels

I see Love whenever I gaze into my little Sister's eyes

The glow from her face when she smiles

Is what gave me this angle

I thank God for sending me this Angel

You know it's real when our mom's name is Angel

Now every woman I see is an Angel

Nicole's story

I used to see this girl

I can't front I thought she was the world

Black Panther Queen

Wasn't just lost in her looks,

But also, in her Heart, Mind, and Soul.

I'd even bet her singing could make Angels glee

When I held her, it felt like she was holding me

But one day she told me her pain

And made me promise not to let it get to me

The Classic Edition

Pray that you feel this

See'

Life isn't easy for kids growing up on the East Side

Of St. Paul that is

Especially when you're black and from Glenridge

And more Especially when you're a little girl and your daddy is in jail, and your mommy is doing drugs

Now when she goes to stores around the block, she sometimes gets to see the men that used to rape her

She got dreams to leave the Cities and never come back. And how could I blame her?

All I could ever think about was how to kill every man that ever hurt her.

But from the traumas of her past,
She stated she doesn't know to Love me.

Cause she doesn't know how Love with a man is supposed to be like, feel like, dreamlike.

She hates when I kiss her and leave her lonely

Even if I'm planning on seeing her that evening

One day she broke to me' You don't really know me

I snapped back' I Love you, so that's the end of story!

With raindrop like tears leaking she murmured'

I swear you hear me but never listen,
How do you Love me when I don't even Love me?

Back In The Day (Not A Kid Anymore)

During my adolescence

I always thought after I'd graduate high school
that I would make it to the pros

Even took acting classes for when I'd retire and
flip a script

Can you imagine how my pride sank when I
never left the bench?

America, can you please tell me what's a black
boys destiny

When none of his role models are sponsored by a
college degree?

I mean we can't all be president

Can someone please tell me how we're supposed
to save the present kids?

I mean we can't all make the league

Trappers telling me' Just chase the green

But when did our creed go from feed to greed?

This is an ode to the things they don't teach

Dreams you got to dig deep to reach

The Classic Edition

Seeds

What do you want to be when you grow up?

I want to be a lawyer!

Really why is that?

Because my dad was a lawyer

How old are you, kid?

I'll be 11 on June 23

And you really want to be a lawyer when you grow up?

Yeah! My Dream is to be just like my Dad!

Nostalgia's Curse (Way Back When)

The youth is the future tell me, have you yet peeped it?

If so, then what are you doing to reach the Dreams you used to Dream of?

Cause growing up hasn't cracked up to what we used to Dream of

Wishing we could go back, but to grow, we got to let go

It's not fair, but that's the way life flows

They say too much nostalgia is bad for our souls

Because it's an addiction and some will sell their souls

Just to live it once more

The Lost Letter (Nobody's Perfect)

Here's a secret

I wanted to die before I met you

That's why I can't live without you

The Light of my Heart

The reason it's still beating

The reason I'm still breathing

And when I do die, if I don't see you in heaven

Like Adam, bet I'm leaving

Make a way to hell lay next to your ashes

You know what? real recognize real

I'd ask God for us to trade places

Take all your pain away

Just glimpse of your smile

Would give me the strength to withstand the rain

You know my Love for you baby

Words can't even paint the frame

The Classic Edition

Me Against The World Part 4 (Heavy In The Game)

Devil wants my soul in exchange for the world

My signature on a contract is all I got to give to receive

When he looks into my eyes

I know he sees the void

See for forty days and nights

I've been trapped in a valley of chills

Push me to edge

There's nothing from which I fear

Matter fact, I'll take the last step off the cliff myself.

Look in my eyes, see the old me is long and dead

He drowned in a river of blood...
That gushed out from a cut to his heart

Feeling like I was crossing the Red Sea
Only to be washed away to awaken on troubles side

How did I fail?
Was it a mistake to embark on a quest to double Love?

Shared Pain

Why do we kill one another?

Some say it's from the thrill of the chase

But I don't want to believe that

Because that would mean we kill for the thrills

And, that's a pain that's hard to heal...

Yes, they say' Revenge is the best for cure the ill

But if more brothers packed steels

That would just mean more wills

More mamas bawling to the heavens wailing'

Is this your will?

(Break)

It's a dog eat dog world to make it to the top

Or so I've heard

So, be ready to dispose any and all in your way

No remorse for where the strays might spray

No regards for the life you'll take

Tell me what numbs the pain?

The Classic Edition

Right Here Models

When my hat is flipped backward, my cousin follows
So, is an eleven-year-old a thug to now do you follow?

(Break)

If it takes a village to raise a child, then our success
is predicated on the Love we give each other

(Break)

This is dedicated to all the parents working doubles
to keep their children's stomachs from growling

When the greatest nourishment
Is the Love from their presence

Great Again (Ashy To Classy)

Once upon a time in history

I heard Irish people weren't white

Funny cause almost every white person I know
has told me what percentage of Irish they are

But if you have one drop of African blood
Boo Hoo, you're black

Then some Arabs born in certain African
countries are labeled white

And some Asians have sued the American
government to be white, google if you doubt

It's funny cause once upon a time in history

I heard Italian people weren't white

Can we get like Sherlock to solve this absurdity?

The Classic Edition

Segregated Eating (2012)

Never knew when I would sit by my black friends at lunch, I was practicing segregation

They were just who I could relate to better without a need for an orientation

And we weren't shunning each other
All our lunches were free

We didn't have a care in the world
The motto was' Brothers let's feast!

Selasie put me on game bout, adding hash browns inside my chicken patty to marinate a little soul into the treat.

The lesson learned

Enjoy every minute that life brings

Cause when that bell rang, and I went back to class

I went back to being lonely

Surely this couldn't have been Martin Luther's Dream

I guess I could have made some white friends

But being their token wasn't my Dream.

Eyes (R.I.P. Emmitt Till)

She stalks me with a spiteful gaze

Like I'm the one that's unmannered

I guess she expects I'm a savage

Because if Brothers don't bow down

They must have an I.Q. below average

Swear the pain their gaze brings to my soul

I admit some days it's hard to manage

It builds the kind of hostility in me that makes
me want to run the streets and ravage

All because I got black skin with a hoodie on
while rocking a hat backward

Sadly, looks do kill cause discrimination still
runs rampant

But allow me to give you a different scenario for
your Hearts to imagine

If leggings and crop tops aren't meant to lead on

Then why when I'm in my black skin
You can't help but fear me?

The Classic Edition

Guilty As US

How do they get heat in the trap?

I heard Richard Nixon put ice in the hood

So, if blacks are the robbers of their jewels

Who is the getaway driver that brought us to our vaults?

Cause America's law says their guilty as us

But somehow, we bare all of the fault

When America's law says their guilty as us

When America's law says their guilty as U.S.

Miss America (She Knows)

I know Malcolm said' By any means necessary

But If I believe in love, would I ever need to
strong-arm someone to make them mine? Been
contemplating lately if our relationship is even
worth the time, we're coming up on four
hundred years together and nothing has changed
like I'm still not worth a dime like my skins still
a crime like since 1619 all I've had is trouble on
my mind

I don't need you to lust me. I need you to Love
me. The difference is in how you treat me. I'm
saying stop and frisk why you always pick me?
But still, you take my pain as a joke, but weren't
you the one who brought me in chains to your
new world? And that pain, do I not still hold?

But no more holding on to the pain with these
words I let go, Miss America, who are you
without your soul?

Ok, I'm done side stepping, I'll say what I'm
trying to say, I think it'll be best if we go our
separate ways, maybe then you'll see who for
you was always there.

The Classic Edition

Good Kid

I heard every night in a ghetto a mother cries

The street corner is where her child's lifeless body lies

I hate having that image pastured in my mind

But we're the ones doing the crime

Well "bad" cops do it too

But I guess they don't really do the time

But I mean we're in Babylon

Did we really expect things to change over time?

We're more worried about martial law

Than upholding moral law

I'm saying If we stopped squeezing nines

Unity is what we'll find!

Just because we're hard-headed doesn't mean we got to be cold-hearted. I'm not from the hood, but what happens in ghetto streets surprisingly influences suburban lives, see we're in an interconnected world where that what affects one directly will also affect others indirectly. There can't be two classifications for the Black peoples of this country, but to be honest, there shouldn't be any classification for any group of people in this world. On the eve of Dr. Martin Luther King's Jr assassination, he gave a most prophetic speech. He cited the children of Israel and their exodus from Egypt, he said, and I quote, "Whenever Pharaoh wanted to prolong the period of slavery in Egypt, he had a favorite formula for doing it. What was that? He kept the slaves fighting among themselves, but whenever the slaves get together, something happens in Pharaoh's court, and he cannot hold the slaves in slavery. When the slaves get together, that's the beginning of getting out of slavery."

Mad City

By the Mississippi River

There we sat down

And we wept, as we remembered Africa

But really it was Zion that we wanted

That's salvation because we realized we're always being hunted

I asked the Lord once' Why are we always haunted?

Got a reply back' Because you're always stunting

That last line holds the answer to anything you've ever wanted.

May Brings Flowers (The Rise)

If this is too deep for the outro

I'll find another use

But just in case it's perfect

Let me introduce

Just another young Brother trying to make it

Don't know how many times I've got to repeat it

But maybe I should just say' A slave trying to get free so that you feel me

Passion's gone, but the drive's still alive

Look in my eyes and see where my Heart resides

If this is too deep for the outro

Then welcome to my demise

But just in case it's perfect

Let me introduce you to my arise

Raise hellfire whenever I arrive

I thought I told you that this drive will never die.

The Classic Edition

ACT 3:

BACK

TO

THE GO

The Roses That Grew From Fire

May I tell you a tale?

It's a story of roses that came from the jungle

Legend says they were planted by Holy Angels

And watered down by tears of joy from Heaven

Seeds truly blessed for their ancestor's good deeds

But to whom much is given much more is expected

So, they were plucked from where they were planted and brought to a land in which they were branded

Where they were forced to work, however, they were commanded, in a living hell is where they thought themselves stranded.

(Break)

At the time of this poem, it's been 153 years since they've been unbranded

But not before Babylon's wealth was greatly expanded

I myself was brought to this land in which my ancestors extended

But now to take advantage of what my Brothers now take for granted

(Opportunity)

But in my quest, I learned emancipation isn't always handed

The brand is now mentally implanted

Buried "Treasures"

I'm from a country you've never heard of

Probably because you never cared too

Because public schools never cared to teach you

But only if you knew all the resources, it brings you

(Break)

Lately, I've been examining life

Through some clearer lenses

Which has brought me to my senses

To write to you this census

So, please double read this sentence

We can't have world peace if you don't care about us!

All I want to say is'

That they don't really care about us!

We're the savages but your race for phones

Is what's causing all the killings over here

Every snapshot is a concealed gunshot

This is a callout for all the kids

Bragging after Christmas about what they got

Now you know each upgrade is a village lost.

The Classic Edition

Congo Day

Congo-born but American raised

Pardon me whenever I'm lost in my American ways

Heard home is where the Heart is

But from Congo, I've sailed away

So, may I reminisce on my childhood memories before they're blown away?

Please allow me to paint to you a picture of a Congo day

On the dirt roads is where my friends and I would play

Imagine an all-black neighborhood, and we aren't worried about strays

We'd even wave at cops passing

Cause our skins color doesn't mean shame

See so when I'm labeled a minority in America

Back home in Congo is where I wish I'd stayed

But Love revealed to me one day

Life isn't all fun and games

Though I must never forget the land from which I came

My Heart is also bonded to serve the world in which We share.

Dear Mama

I Love you, Mama

I couldn't imagine a better line to start this poem

Cause from you my whole life came to a start

The only women there for me from the very start

An African Queen

Who came to America and had to restart

I know it felt like a shot to your pride

But God willing you never let things fall apart

So, from my Heart, you'll never depart

Words can't describe

What your presence means to my life

So, I'll just end this with the best line

To come to my heart

I Love you, Mama
The Classic Edition

Africa's Go

Have you ever felt as if half of you were missing?

As if it were on the other side of the world

But your smile doesn't really show, that there's something bubbling in your soul, so your pain nobody really knows?

Made it to America but had to leave my Brothers in the Go, made it in America but forgot my Brothers in the Go

I was only 6 when I had to go, so I'm not labeling the blessing I've been bestowed as a woe, so please don't misquote

It's just since I've gotten older it has become a burden to me, so my minds been on Jim crow, segregating my thoughts like what to my Sisters and Brothers do I really owe?

Got the world whispering in my ear' You were the one chosen, so homie get the dough. Work hard to move your family to a state where it doesn't snow and just let everybody else go

But then a light switches in my Heart, like but them my family from the Go, least I could say is hello, know you haven't seen me since I was a little boy

Are you proud of the way I've grown? Because I'm a product of the world we've sown I know words can't fill the void

So, please allow me to show you my Heart is forever yours

I Am

I am a lost child in the Congo who watched his village get bombed by drones so the world could obtain the minerals beneath my people's feet, I am a child soldier from Sierra Leone who was forced to pull the trigger on the rifle which sent my parents to their grave, I am the orphaned children working 14 hours shifts in communist China's factories for a wage that barely keeps us above starving, I am a kidnapped 7-year-old Brazilian girl whose sold to the highest bidder to have my innocence taken from me, I am the daughter of a father who never let me hear his voice, I am the memory of a college-bound high school senior who fell victim to a stray a week before graduation, I am a nightmare, but yet I am with the youth. Therefore I am the future.

The Classic Edition

The Return of Simba

I got Dreams that if you ever meet anyone from my village

They'll tell you that I'm their brother

Call us Queens and Kings

Because the life of Simba is what we're living

Not talking Hakuna Matata, but the real rebellion

We're the risen children of a genocide never written about in school textbooks

Search The free state of Congo to find out what Léopold's freedom means

Then let those images sink in like the blades them Belgium terrorist used to set an example

See what we don't know can and will hurt us

What we don't learn from the past is bound to return

And who do you think the shackles will be bound to when it returns?

Babylon's Shame

I used to be ashamed to of been born in Africa

I would say with pride that I was raised in Babylon

See in Babylon if you go the same color on it doesn't mean you're guaranteed to get along

I know it may seem like I'm babbling on, but it's true me and blacks didn't always get along

Looked the part but what was different was my name

So, to them, I wasn't real enough because to them my roots weren't deep enough

So, there I was a confused slave wishing to share in my sibling's pain by being disgraced that my grandparents saw Babylon's ships but were taken on another route.

The Classic Edition

Congo Lights

I lay in my father's arms

My head pressed upon his chest

His heartbeat sings to me a lullaby

As my eyes come to a rest

(Break)

I know I haven't lived the perfect life that my father envisioned, can't hang my head low though

I heard every mistake you own up to is just a splash of water to regain your vision

Now I'm not saying my wrongs helped me write these psalms. I'm saying my wrongs helped me right these psalms.

See there's only one place to go when you're at the bottom, so I pray each letter I scribe is a climb closer to my Dreams

If these words paint you a picture

I pray the image it projects is Love is You

(Break)

I lay in my father's arms

My head pressed upon his chest

His heartbeat sings to me a lullaby

As my soul comes to a rest

ACT 4:

FREEDOM

FIGHTERS

The New Stars

What cause makes a Freedom Fighter? Taxation without representation?

Well tell the world we're fighting entrapment without documentation

Write it in your newspapers that we're fighting political degradation

Project it on your news channels that we're fighting governmental oppression

Speak of it on your radios that we're fighting economical exploitation

All while you label us terrorists, as you torture us asking us' Why we hate America?

But in reality, we're fighting to make America finally Love us.

The Bonus Army (99 Percent)

Long as European decedents claim to be white in America, I'll forever remain a second-class citizen

Don't expect an apology from me. You're in the majority, of course, I expect you to see it different

Pardon me for addressing a white audience like they'll actually read me; I'm just saying if they listened they would feel me

Cause all I'm doing is repeating what my ancestors told me
This is King Kunta never mistake me for toby

The Freedom Party

Now I'm no politician

But I am a part of a Freedom party

Think Glory, Runaway slaves returned fighting men.

Better yet imagine Malcolm walking beside Martin, with Huey P right behind chanting out loud' Turn up!

So, let this be our message to the nation from the grassroots

The Prelude to the Revolution is here

Meaning Love Shall be achieved

By any Loving means necessary

So, just sit back and receive
The Classic Edition

Compromised

Hey, Mr. Officer, can I live?

Cause this chokehold you got me in is kind of making it hard for me to breath

I know stop and frisk is the law

But are we to it the only ones to whom it applies?

Please don't shoot me

I'm not saying I'm not trying to comply

I'm just saying this is the third time this month I've been confined

And not once have you guys found what you wish to find

I was just wondering if we could please re-compromise

Because this three-fifths stuff is getting kind of odd

Cause the only thing you guys seem to ever find

Is the truth you so wish to hide.

Kin (Lean On Me)

If I lived in 1852

I'd be a runaway slave

Who returns south

A conductor for the Underground Railroad

If I lived in 1961

I'd be packed in a jail cell with my Sisters and Brothers

As we sing to the Heavens above us'

We Shall Overcome

If I lived in 2020

I'd be marching in every ghetto American street

Chanting out loud to all my Sisters and Brothers'

When one of us wins, we all taste Victory!

Or have you forgotten that you are Kin to me?

The Classic Edition

The New Emancipation Proclamation

Their mission plan is that we never see admissions

So, I question your intuition

Because you can't learn that in their institutions

Can't even blame you because they don't even give us a real education

Walk into a school cafeteria I'll bet you'll still see segregation

Ask them about slavery I bet they'll still give you no real explanation

Am I wrong for feeling like I'm living in a world where they're scheming on our extermination?

That's why my mind stays on our emancipation

If not us, then our future generation

But this time will be sure to take all our reparations

Love To Me

What's freedom to me?

When we stop dreaming of being trappers

What's freedom to me?

When children of former slave owners and slaves sit equally at the same table

What's freedom to me?

When ghettos cease to exist

What's freedom to me?

I said it before and I'll say it again'

Freedom to me is Love

The New Era

They say the youth isn't really a part of this world

I said that's the truth cause we still believe in Love

Look to the sky, don't hate, tell me we don't look fly?

This is the 60's renewed, but this time we got our degrees

Bout to put mine on a congress man's chest

And let him feel the heat

Change is going to come, and here it is

We're the Hope in a hopeless world

Please observe as all we do is win.

The Classic Edition

13th Amendment

Hey, Mr. President, won't you let my people go?

It's been 400 years, haven't we made this country enough dough?

What more could you ask of us we're the ones broke?

You put us in ghettos, so we're the ones coked

Babylon's glory is well known to the world

So, what more is needed from the enslavement of us folks?

All we want is to be free so that we can Dream of Hope

That's freedom for our weary souls.

Free .99

They say the chills you get from the thrills heals

So, let these words be my Dreams and not my will

Cause freedom can't arise from a bill

And It's a long fall from the top of capitol hill

I'm just saying, can we get some leaders that have missed a few meals?

I think they might be better suited to understand how we feel.

Turf War

There's a war outside

Red vs. Blue

What side are you clinging too?

Or did your street make you?

Maybe your pops was with it too?

Or are you independent

Cause the foolish games aren't you?

There's a war outside

Red vs. Blue

Both out for the loot

Quick to pull the trigger and shoot

Both claim they'll never call truce

But yet they're both getting paid by the same dudes in the black suits

There's a war outside

Reblooblicans vs. Democrips

Voting starts soon in a city near you

The Classic Edition

Unity

This is for all my Sisters and Brothers in the struggle

Color no longer applies to me

We're all bonded by the same shackles mentally

Look how they've perpetuated our mentality

Cause now we chase money irrationally

Just to stunt in chains and whips

How did we get to this slavery?

What's the point of fitting in a world that doesn't motivate you internally?

It's not like you can stay on earth for eternity

Up Next

They say when the truth sinks in it hurts

That's why the truth bringer usually ends up in a hearse

Life hits you once nobody gets a second chance to rehearse

Reason some of us live life in reverse

Cause when we see life evil is all we observe

That's why some are like' Why the wealthy got it all and we're the ones always getting curved?

To live young, wild, and free, we too should deserve!

But if only they knew to the humble is to whom Love is reserved

The Classic Edition

Unity Part 2

The person I see in the mirror is my greatest enemy

He's the only one that can lead me down a path of misery

He's the only one that can tarnish my legacy

That's why I pray to never deviate from my destiny

I'm speaking of the day I'll receive life's greatest remedy

That's Dreams of an Eternity of Serenity.

Superstars

Got Dreams to shine a light

That helps point a road home to the world's lost souls

Because a lost soul is but a diamond in disguise

And a star shines the brightest upon the night sky

So, allow Love to be the light that leads you home

See-through Love there's life

It heals the oppressed

While the oppressors think themselves swell

But know Caesar's coin

Doesn't grant wishes for all to be well

So, please open your Heart up to Love

And allow It to save you from where you dwell

The Classic Edition

The Fighting Spirit

I think I'm in danger

Been acting out in anger

Lately, life's been playing out like scrabble

I'm trying to scramble, but I keep getting sacked

And I don't believe in fourth-down punting

Because I'm done being patient

Been done waiting for my miracle

If time is money

Then I'm going to need at least nine figures

Outlaws

The world thought we would never be re-seen

But here we are bursting like a new-found spring

This is that cooling water to cool boiling water

The salt to give the world a little bit more flavor

This is the harvest from the mustard seeds

That landed on fertile soil

Now observe as schemes uncoil

See our new motto is don't worry

Be happy

Because now all we think to ourselves

Is' What a wonderful world

So, won't you help me sing again

The songs of Freedom

The Classic Edition

Don't Let Go (Conquerors)

I'd be lying if I said' I never thought of making it to primetime

But I got to stay true to my roots I'm talking grassroots

If you want to know what we're preaching

Its Love pass it on

I didn't come to lead you I came to walk beside you

So, if you trip I'll offer a helping hand

I just pray you to do the same if I too shall slip

We're not perfect that's the truth

But who wrote the rule that we can't aspire to be

Serenity is the only thing I'm conspiring to see

That's why in this life I'm inspired to be all that I can be

I'm not trying to sell you a Dream

See inspirations are free

I'm just trying to reach the kids that wonder if they have a reason to live

By showing them Love

So, they have no more reasons to grieve

ACT 5:

STRAIGHT

OUTTA

GO

(THE PAIN OF LOVE)

August 1st, 1784

After a grueling three-week voyage, the ship, to which I have been granted permission to board, has finally anchored at port Luanda off the central west coast of the continent of Africa. Well, at least from what I could hear earlier this morning from the screams of some of the crewmen on deck announcing preparation start being made for our anchoring. Before I continue, allow me to take a moment to make everything clear to whoever might find themselves reading this diary.

Now I'm no sailor; my name is Danial MacAleese. I am the son of a wealthy English tobacco salesman named Sir Albert Middleton. The reason I do not bear the same name as that of my father is due to my mother being Irish. I was the bastard child of my father's youth, as the English love to call us Irish who are born to them out of wedlock. Growing up, I never had the opportunity to meet or know anything of my father. Whenever I would make an inquiry of him to my mother, she would scold me by telling me we don't exist in his life, so neither will he in ours. I was raised by my mother's family, who are sheepherders in Belfast, Northern Ireland. My mother's family is not very wealthy; still, they have provided me with unconditional love and have never made me feel any different from the rest of the family due to who my father is.

But for this diary, I will skip over the details of my youth because if you are from Belfast, we have more than likely experienced the same youthful adventures, meaning we can share many similar stories. So, with that, I will only retrace in this diary the events which have led me to this day.

On April 21st of the year 1784, the day of my 22nd birthday, I received a letter from my father dated December 27th, 1783, by way of Charleston, South Carolina. In this letter, my father told me of his successful exploits in the new world we have all come to know as America; he informed me of how he has doubled his wealth by way of his plantation, where cotton is picked making him now not only a tobacco salesman but also a very profitable cotton trader. To make a long story short, he requested my presence as an overseer at his plantation and has guaranteed me riches of my wildest imagination for my mother's family and myself. Though my mother protested to the idea of me going, the rest of the family agreed that this was a great blessing. The money that I will be able to send back to them from working in America for my father for just a year will be more than I could earn working in Belfast for five years.

Now I must admit, I am not the ripest fruit hanging from a tree; I have not received the type of education most English youth who have a wealthy father will receive, but I will do my best to detail my adventures in this diary as best as I can. My schooling has come from my grandfather, William MacAleese, and my uncle, Arthur MacAleese, through books that they managed to get their hands on along the course of their lives. As I was growing up, they would always tell me that I would be special and that I have an anointing coming my way. They used that as a reason to more firmly tutor me than they would my cousins, forcing me to do and additional reading after the daily lessons they would give all of us.

To continue with how I arrived at my current interval in life; My father, being the profitable merchant, he is, arranged for me to board one of his ships at a port in London. But unfortunately, instead of going straight to America as I had hoped, we would. First, we would have to make a stop at a port named Luanda off the Central West Coast of the continent of Africa to pick up some slaves; this is the port I believe we're anchored to. But after the pickup, the ship will deliver the slaves to another port in Charleston, South Carolina, along with me; from there, we will make way to my father's plantation.

I would have begun writing in my diary of my adventures during the first day that I set sail from the port in Dublin. But unfortunately, that very day not more than three hours offshore, I got seasick. The last thing I can remember of that day was collapsing on deck, then staring at the vast blue sky as darkness began to consume my vision.

My being seasick thus has had me confined to my quarters on bed rest since that day. I have yet to receive the opportunity to meet and make a proper introduction of myself to the crew to which I will be sailing with to America. Well, other than the young lad who has been nursing me since my ship exchange. To who I'm sure wasn't on the first ship I boarded at the port in Dublin, because the whole crew from that ship had cheerfully greeted me on deck when I first came abroad, and I don't remember his face from any of the men to which I met.

My sickness, to say the least, has been very displeasing. Always being around family has made the isolation to which I'm confined to be quite a discomforting. And not being able to enjoy the sea and explore this magnificent ship after the slight glimpse I was able to muster as I was carried on board on my presumed death mat during my ship exchange at the port in London, has been soul-wrenching. Though I am saddened by this sickness, which has taken the first three weeks of my voyage to my new life away from me, if it is as my grandfather says that good things come to those that wait, then the weight I shall receive shall be well-plenty.

The Classic Edition

Due to this being the first morning I have found enough strength to leave my quarters and walk about the ship, I first thought I should write of all the events that have brought me to this point. I do not know the next time I will make an account of my life in this diary. Still, I promise it will be soon so that all of you kids in Belfast to whom will ever find yourself reading this will know that we the Irish can rise from the dust and become something of ourselves in this world where we're told that we're nothing. I cannot begin to write to you of how excited I am to leave my quarters and see the world; my heart sings with jubilee, as I could have never wished for such a wondrous blessing, which has befallen to me.

Danial MacAleese
August 1st, 1784

DREAMS

The Classic Edition

August 3rd, 1784

On the morning of August 1st, I thought myself blessed as if I awoke to a dream come true; little did I know I had awoken to a nightmare. Before I give details of that horrid morning and the events that followed, I shall tell you of the man that led my eyes to the greatest tragedy to which I believe has been bestowed upon human beings. After signing my name in my diary, I leaped to my feet and didn't even bother returning it to my pack as I hurried to the door leading to the rest of the ship. I was bursting with extreme joy to meet the crew to which I had hoped would become something like brothers to me, given that we would be spending the next months of our lives together at sea.

But as soon as I opened the door leading to what I had hoped would be a wonderful future, there the man stood blocking my path. He was clothed in all black from his boots to his hat, and to add spice to his grimacing look, and he had a dark brown beard with strides of gray hair that stretched down to the top of his chest. Before I could introduce myself to him on our first meeting, he bowed before me, and spoke in an eloquent but profane manner as he said, "Captain Donald Arrington at, your service." I have often heard tales of pirates pillaging in the Caribbean; granted, I have never seen one of these notorious men with my own eyes, but

I'm sure captain Donald Arrington fit the description of what a pirate looked like as told to me. Mainly by way of the tales I hear from travelers who pass through pubs in Belfast.

After our sterile introduction, the captain immediately asked for my presence in his quarters. Though I envied to see the world outside, I was in no position to decline the captain's invitation. His chambers were located down the hall from mines and the rest of the crews. And as we entered the captain's quarters, my eyes beheld for the first time Africans. Two women to be exact, both lying naked on his bed, each with a chain attached to their left ankle locked to hooks wedged to the ground near the legs of the bed. Both women wept bitterly as we entered the room, and then proceeded to hold each other tightly when both the captains and I's gazes became solely focused on them.

Before a thought could enter my mind to make something of this situation, it was briskly blocked out by a loud bark to the two women, from the captain to which he screamed out, 'You dirty whores! Show some respect when your master walks in the room'. Then he looked back to me with a malicious smile and offered myself to them. I refused and used my ill health as an excuse in fear of his response to my rejection of his offer, yet though he insisted, I continued to protest, and after a few more attempts, he finally gave in to my unwillingness.

After a few seconds upon his finally accepting my decision had passed, with a loud shout, he called three crewmen to the room. We had a minor introduction. Then captain Arrington gave orders to them that continue to haunt me till this very hour, "Men take these two wenches to the crew's chambers and let the boys have their fill of fun before the new cargo comes in, and when their finished, throw these things overboard so the sea creatures may feast as well." Never in my life have I seen nor heard such barbarianism in my presence. All I could do was stand still as I watched the man obey the orders given to them to unchain and take the women away. All I could do was stand still as I heard the women screaming in terror; all I could do was stand still as I watched the tears rolling down from their cheeks fall to the ground like heavy raindrops as they struggled to free themselves from the men, unfortunately though to no avail. It was difficult for me even to utter a single thought in my mind as all this occurred, and as they left the room, I struggled to hold back the shaking that began to engulf my body. I swear to you their cries were like stab wounds to my soul.

Then before I could regain my composure from what I had just witnessed, there came from the corner of my ear, "Danial, don't feel pity for these beasts of the world; if God intended for them to be human, then we wouldn't rule over them as we do now. You'll see soon enough that these things are not men nor women, but an object of our use in which we may choose to do to them whatever we so, please. It might be hard for your Irish tilled brain to comprehend what I am saying to you fully. But you are also half English, so you are, in a sense, sane. You see, I am employed by your father, who is a godly anointed shepherd to guide you and teach you on this journey, granted I don't share his sense of religion, but I do share his sense of mastery of power over these beasts".

He then grabbed me by my shoulder and led me to a table with chairs on opposite sides of each other; he first sat me down on the chair to which would be mine before making way to his. After taking his time to posture himself in his chair, he continued with his declaration stating, "Your father owns one of the biggest and wealthiest plantations in South Carolina. Although he is married and has children of full English blood, he couldn't help but feel obliged to tend to his bastard son; apparently, it is something God told him to do". After saying this, he took a brief moment to laugh at the statement. Then continuing, "Again, as I said, that's why I don't share his sense of religion." He then sat forward, looked me in the eyes and asked, "Do you know why you weren't just put on a boat directly to America, but instead, first, you were brought to this God-forsaken land? I see from the look of fear in your eyes that you don't". At this, I couldn't look him in the face anymore; all I could do was drop my head and murmur to him, "No." I could feel his delight at my being at his mercy. "Because your job at your father's plantation will be as an overseer. Just as you were tending sheep in whatever intolerant village, you came from in Ireland. You will now be tending hairless sheep in America. So, you see, I guess you will still be working with animals in a sense. Our purpose here, other than to deliver the cargo to your father, is also to prepare you for the work you will be doing at your father's plantation. There is no better way to do this than to put you directly in contact with the beasts before and during the breaking process".

Then just right before another word could leave his tongue, one of the three crewmen from before, to whom was introduced to me as first mate Roger Williams, broke into the room excessively sweaty and breathing extremely heavily. The captain broke his gaze from me to first mate Rogers upon his entry. He then raised his hand to him with his palm up. His way of giving him the floor to speak. After a few seconds of trying to catch his breath, the first mate finally said to him, "Pardon me for my interruption, but the cargo is at the docks awaiting your order to be brought in." I caught a slight smile pass through captain Arrington's lips as he stood to the first mate's pronouncement. The captain then glared to me and commanded I followed him, assuring me we would be finishing our conversation at a later time. So, I did as he ordered and followed him and first mate Rogers to the ship's deck.

As my head made contact with the outside world for the first time in three weeks, it was met by a humidity that I had never experienced; soon after, though, it was accompanied by a cool soothing breeze that massaged away the anguish produced by the hot sun. Upon fully submerging my body onto the deck of the ship and fully engulfing myself in the heat, my ears were quickly intruded by the sounds of clinking iron. As I fixated my eyes to see where the sounds were coming from. I began to shake uncontrollably to what I saw before me; men, women, and children chained from their necks to their ankles. Each with a second chain subduing their arms locked to their wrist. All were walking in pairs of two onto the ship.

I could not get a full headcount of how many of them were to enter the ship, but I believe there could not have been less than a hundred of them. Then for a second time, on that day before a single thought could enter my mind to make something of the situation, it was intruded by an order from captain Arrington, who told me to follow him to what he detailed as to where the cargo enters to welcome them. At this order, I could no longer feel my legs under me. How I was able to comply and follow him still to this hour of this very day, I do not know.

While standing beside captain Arrington as the slaves were boarded onto the ship, I couldn't help but notice the frightened look of uncertainty beaming from their faces. My heart was sunken, and the only thought that lingered in my mind as I was seeing all this unfold before me was to question what these people could have done to deserve the condition they were abiding in. All of them were clothed in nothing but sackcloth trousers, making it that every one of them was bare-chested, including the women and children. To make matters worse as the slaves were passing by captain Arrington and me, the captain slapped the ones he believed weren't moving fast enough to his liking, on the back of their head. The women and children were not excluded from this. And as he struck them, he would scream out all sorts of slander to belittle them, words that I wish not to repeat.

As the last of the slaves were being boarded on, out of nowhere, one stumbled on an unhinged plank and fell to his knees in front of me. He was a young male who looked in healthier shape than most of the other slaves that I saw brought on onto the ship. I acted without a moment's thought and gave out my hand to him to help him to his feet. While rising with my aid, he forces our eyes cross paths, and during the interlock exchange, he passes me a nod; but as I looked into his eyes, I did not see fear as I saw in the eyes of some of the other passing slaves. I will add though most of the slaves were avoiding looking in my direction to which had captain Arrington at my side who was as I said slapping and cursing slaves to whom he believed weren't moving fast enough.

To proceed, before I could return any gesture to the man whose eyes had no fear, my right cheek quickly grew warm; and as soon as I knew it, I fell to the deck floor. The center of my left cheek was the first part of my body to make contact with the splintery wood surface. Not knowing what had occurred, I flipped to my back to see where the blow had come from, and immediately, I realized that captain Arrington had struck me. Then as I readied myself to crawl away from him, he steps over me, trapping me in between his legs. Then leaning over me, he began screaming and hurling all types of profanity that belittle us, Irish, terms I am sure we have all heard from our interactions with not just the English but with other Europeans as well, words that I wish not to repeat.

After his insults ceased, he ordered to have me flogged, but quickly resented that order, and commanded for me to be confined to my quarters for the rest of the day until he figured out what to do with me. Such was an order I humbly complied with. I saw it a blessing to be away from the monstrosities that I was witnessing not only on this ship but also around the whole port, at least from as far as my eyes would let me see.

I wanted to write in my diary that night, but I could not get the images of the poor Africans being boarding onto the ship out of mind, as well as thoughts of the fate of the two women I saw chained to captain Arrington's bed. I also could not write due to my ears not being able to block out the heinous sounds of the crew, to whom I am now sure to be pirates, laughing of their folly as I heard them berating the slaves in the lower compartments of the ship. I spent my night immobilized by the fear that I might also end up sharing the Africans fate.

The following morning, I awoke to a summons to captain Arrington's quarters by a crewman who banged and screamed the information to me outside my door. As I entered in for the second time to what I had concluded the night before to be the tomb of

Satan himself, I saw two women sitting next to each other on the captain's bed. Both on the side facing the door, opposite to the side to which would make it that they would be sitting facing captain Arrington to whom was sited at his chair. Returning to the two women, I saw as I entered the room. They were incredibly calm when I looked upon them, unlike the two women from yesterday who trembled at my gaze, expecting what I assumed only the worst from me. And as I stared closer at them and thoughts of their fate begin to circulate in my head, I noticed one of them to be quite young. I'm sure she could not have been past her teenage years. A cold feeling started to develop in my stomach as my mind finally came to a resolution at the extent of the captain's tyranny.

Before I could pull my mind from the dark abyss of his capabilities, the captain called to me from across the room, leaning back on his chair "You cannot have these ones; the crew can't touch new cargo until we leave the dock, teaches them discipline." After this declaration, he then ordered me to sit with him at his table, and without hast, I made my way to the chair he had sat me in the previous day. But unlike the day before, where we sat across from each other. As soon as I sat down, the captain walked over to my side and took a seat on the table, so to be right in my face.

The Classic Edition

Then before he began speaking, he removed a small bottle of rum from his coat pocket, to which he took a long pull that emptied it. After he had guzzled its last drops, he threw the bottle with all the might he could muster in the direction of the door but only to hit the wall a few steps from its left side. The two women and I all shuttered as the bottle shattered. But after a moment, we all reverted to being calm. I can say I felt as if the two women's energy of calmness was passed on to me because after the captain had struck me the other day, I thought I could never face him again. That's why I say seeing the posture of those two women who I knew to be in a worst situation than I, be so calm gave me slight confidence, well in this case enough that was needed to face the captain.

To add, the two women that I saw on this day, as I noted prior, were more clam than the two women chained to the captain's bed the day before. And after the captain's bottle hurl, I realized they reminded me of the same man who I had helped the other day to his feet. But, before my mind could linger deeper in this thought, I felt a gentle slap to my cheek and saw captain Arrington's gaze focused solely on me. Then with his now to me classic evil smirk, he repeated, "The crew is not allowed to touch the new cargo until we leave the dock. But do *not worry; soon, we will leave this ratchet continent where God sends his cursed".*

He followed this statement up by resetting himself on top of the table. He then continued by delivering to me the most crippling unholiest sermon of all-time. One that I believe Satan himself gives to his demons at the lowest level of hell. I wish not to repeat all the folly he said to me. I do not want to contaminate anyone's soul with the ills that this man had to say. The way he swayed and bent the scripture to justify his cruelty and lustful desires, I could not understand, nor did I want to follow. I will say the English themselves did not impose such cruelty on us or the Scottish when they had us as serfs as they do to these Africans.

Bringing my summonsed to a close, after his drunken rant, the captain sent me off. As I was making way to leave the room, he called out to me once more and assured me that despite my being the bastard son to his current employer or not, he would kill me the next time I showed compassion to the slaves in his presence. At that, I retreated to my room and again have spent my day in solitude. I want nothing to do with this forsaken crew or ship. I have been praying that I may fall ill once more and not awake until I arrive in America. I apologize for my bluntness, but the atrocity I can hear on this ship is too much to bear. I also relive all that I have seen with each word I write.

Danial MacAleese
August 3rd, 1784

August 6th, 1784

We finally set sail for America on the early morning of the 4th of August. I have yet to leave my chambers since my second meeting with the captain; the same lad who had nursed me while I was ill during the voyage from London to port Luanda has been delivering to me my provisions of food. His name is Charles Twain, and I do say I have grown to become very fond of this young gentleman. Through our conversations, I have come to learn that he's seventeen years of age and a son of a former sailor named Henry Twain, who died while serving under captain Arrington two years ago at sea during a voyage in the Caribbean. Charles told me in captain Arrington's extending mercy to him, an act I wasn't aware the captain was capable of, at least from what I have seen of him.

Nonetheless, to proceed on the captain took Charles the eldest son of Henry Twain as a steward on this here ship to help provide for his family as his father has once done. I did attempt to inquire about how his father died, but Charles wished not to speak of it, so I have never resurfaced the topic since. Other than that, our conversations have had no bounds, and we will usually talk for hours after he delivers my provisions of food or whenever he makes free time from his other duties on the ship.

Charles tells me countless stories he's heard of adventures at sea and his knowledge of the world at large to which have fallen upon his ears.

He also informed me of the types of ships that roam the sea, as well as the creatures that dwell within its depths. I came to discover that our vessel, to which is named Judah, is not even that large compared to other slave ships. Charles detailed to me that we're on board a private delivery ship that can carry no more than 200 slaves a voyage, to whom usually all go to one location, for our journey that being my father's plantation. While other slave ships to whom may all vary in size can carry upwards to 600 slaves on board to be delivered to an auction block to be sold to different owners.

Charles has even told me of my father's plantation and how grand it is; he says that it is budding with wildlife and crops, so no one ever goes hungry, but rather everyone eats to their heart's content. I asked him if the slaves were treated better there than here on this ship, he did not entirely give me an answer but instead changed the topic. Also, while in deep conversation with Charles, I came to learn that he and most of the other men aboard the ship is illiterate. I followed up this revelation by asking Charles how the captain then comes about finding a crew. He responded by telling me it is not very difficult because the captain goes to the poor and offers them wealth, food, and the pleasures of a women's flesh. I told Charles I was dumbstruck by this knowledge, for I thought America was the land of the rich. A land where no one goes hungry, a land where each family has a basket full of abundant opportunity; at least, this seemed to be the case by way of the tales I had been told in Ireland. But Charles rebuked my statement of America's wealth and opportunity by telling me that many people are broke in America and that all a lot of people can do for themselves is work manual labor jobs or be blessed to own a farm. I asked him how a young lad, such as himself came to obtain so much knowledge of the land and world at large, and he responded by telling me that his mother had told him.

I do not know if it was pity or lowliness of mind, but I offered to teach Charles how to read. I informed him, though, that it would take more time for him to learn how to read than we would have together on the ship. Nonetheless, Charles excitingly accepted my offer to teach him how to read. Still, he requested that we not tell anyone what we're doing because he sought this as an opportunity to disband from the ship when we ported in America. To this I asked Charles why he couldn't just freely leave, to which he followed by informing me that when one agrees to work on captain Arrington's ship, they are bound to six years of service and whether it is on land or sea they must obey all of the captain's orders. This made me feel very wary for Charles as I feared only the worst of the deal that he was bound to.

My fear for Charles has made me wearier of my situation. I now understand why my mother kept the knowledge of my father away from me. If men like captain Arrington are whom my father holds in his company, then my father's attitude may not differ from theirs. How now I dread my coming to America. I refuse to be a part of this barbarism, which these people call slavery. In no means am I saying that I am now a righteous man because I have seen the evils of slavery first hand, I did happily accept being an overseer. But my perception of slavery was given to me by my grandfather from the law of Moses. But if the law of Moses were to be applied here, then all the Africans aboard this ship would have to be set free from the injury they are receiving.

How I wish I heeded to my mother's warnings because as I continue to write in this diary, I see now I am on a ship destined to bring me to my death. I fear I am sailing through the valley of the shadow of death.

Danial MacAleese
August 6th, 1784

The Classic Edition

August 10th, 1784

It pains me to write this, but I must detail more of the evils that are occurring on this ship; my heart will not allow me to ignore these atrocious acts any longer and only make accounts in this diary that is as if I am the sole person suffering. After captain Arrington struck me, I have failed to mention all the weeping and gnashing of the teeth I have been hearing coming from beneath me where the slaves are stored. I failed to mention the harsh sounds of hard objects that I do not wish to know what, hitting human flesh. I failed to mention the haunting sounds of women up on the deck or in the crew's quarters, screaming in bitter torment as they fall victim to these monster's lustful desires. This is why I enjoy my conversations with Charles so much. It allows my mind to wander off and temporally subdue the sounds and thoughts of what's going on around me. But selfishly, that's part of why I offered to teach Charles how to read, so that I may be with him longer, as I see him as an escape of reality.

Yet, on this day the 10th of August, I requested Charles. I knew one of his many duties on board this ship is to feed the slaves, So I asked to join him the next time he went. The previous night I had a dream of the two women that I saw in captain Arrington's quarters the second time I was there, the women whose eyes had no fear. Though in one of our prior conversations, Charles had informed me that captain Arrington throws all the women who are victims to his lustful desires overboard. So they do not produce an offspring, just as he had commanded the first time I was in his quarters. But I remembered the man with the same type of fearless eyes as the women who I had helped up after he had fallen by my feet. I felt the dream was a sign that I should see this man, because while I was in fear for my life, this man was not, and he was to be a slave while I was to be his overseer.

To proceed on to what followed upon my request; as we were nearing the entrance to where the slaves were being stored, I began smelling something extremely vile; it grossly plagued my nostrils and made me start coughing bitterly. To this, I quickly plugged my nose with my thumb and forefinger, but this only subsided the smell a little. At this, Charles informed me that you never get used to the scent. Then he asked me if this was what I wanted to see with hopes that I would change my mind. But I firmly responded yes, and we proceeded into the chamber. What my eyes saw, just like everything else on this ship, I still cannot wash away from my mind.

The room was eerily dark, but some light was able to creep in from the cracks in the ceiling. It was also very humid, but what is one to expect in a room where one hundred and more people are being stored. I was surprised, though, that all the slaves were together: the men, women, and children. All bare-chested and still in chains. Some were lying on the ground, and others were sitting with their backs to the walls of the ship. Unfortunately, though, some were also dead; it was all too horrid. Charles told me that in other boats, it is a lot worse as the slaves there have no room and are often confined to one position for the whole voyage. In response, I asked him if these slaves knew then that they were blessed. Charles shrugged at my statement, then proceeded to hand out the provisions to the slaves. I noticed that some would refuse to take it though; I saw in their eyes that they preferred to die of hunger than to go on any further, while others readily accepted the provisions as if it were their last meal.

After observing Charles work for a moment, I started to look for the man with the fearless eyes. I made my way to the back of the room, studying everybody's faces to look into their eyes, but many refused to look at me, and some would hide their face as I walked past them. When I finally got to the butt of the room, I came across a storeroom. I shouted to Charles to ask what was in there, and he shouted back that it was weapons, mostly blades. I asked why captain Arrington would put the weapons and the slaves so close together, and Charles retorted that the slaves were broken and did not know what was in there, so it made no difference. I sighed as he spoke these words, and as I began my turn back to him, I recognized the man with fearless eyes looking right at me, his eyes still seemingly fearless. His back was pressed up against the wall next to the storeroom, but before I could make my way to him, I heard footsteps coming down from the stairs, and I quickly reverted to my prior intentions of walking back to Charles.

Before I was even halfway back to Charles, lo and behold captain Arrington and two other men were in our presence. The captain greeted me with his villainous smile, adding how he was happy that I had finally awoken from my second slumber. Not knowing what to say and in fear for my life, I thanked him. His eyes took a liking to the fear that was radiating off me. He then began to look amongst the slaves intently. I began to fear for the man with the fearless eyes, for I thought that perhaps the captain was looking for him, though I could not imagine what for. But then the captain pointed to two women, and the crew members accompanying him hurried to them. To which was followed by the captain tossing the men the keys to unlock the women. Both of the women screamed in deep terror as they were being taken. Other slaves started to tremble in fear as this was occurring, but none dared tried making any motion towards what was happening. After the two women were secured, captain Arrington and the men he commanded started making their way out the room and up the steps. Bringing the women to what I was sure would be back to captain Arrington's quarters.

I sighed a breath of relief that the men and the captain were gone, but my heart was in agony for the two women chosen. Before I could feel my legs return under me, captain Arrington reappeared and tossed Charles the keys, then told him to give it to first mate Rogers at the helm instructing Charles to tell Rogers to throw the dead overboard and bring the keys back to him for he wished to speak to him. Charles nodded to the captain then right as the captain was about to leave our presence for a second time. Charles called out to him and asked the captain if he could meet with him to speak of a matter that was of great importance to him. The captain first looked at me, then back at Charles, and then readily accepted, telling him to visit his quarters later during the day.

After the captain was finally gone, I asked Charles what it was that he wanted to speak to the captain about. Charles replied that he wanted to ask the captain for leave when we made it to America because they were to set sail for London one week after we arrived in Charleston, and that would not be sufficient time for Charles to spend with his family. It would also provide a way for us to continue his reading lessons with me. I wanted to tell Charles not to make such a request of the captain, for fear of Charles being rejected, but who was I to say to him not to attempt to see his family. So, I quickly changed the conversation, asking Charles if those were the only keys onboard the ship that could free the slaves. He confirmed this, adding a caveat that the keys were only to be used in the presence of the captain or the first mate. I, of course, then inquired why then he would have been given them and not one of the men that the captain came with? Or better yet, why wouldn't the captain just have Charles tell Rogers to visit him to grab the keys? But why did the captain put the keys in Charles's hands unsupervised by him or the first mate?

I apologize for my pause mid-passage, but an event occurred as I was writing that required my immediate attention that forced me to leave my chambers. But to give the story plainly, As I was writing of my inquiry of the keys assigned to Charles, I heard a knock at my door. I quickly covered my diary with some breaches that I had lying around; then, without me even having yet taken a step in the direction of the door, it was thrust open, and there stood first mate Rogers and two other crewmen. First mate Rogers commanded me to follow him to the deck. I inquired why, but he only repeated his order once more. I asked if I could grab a coat because it was the middle of the night, but at this request, first mate Rogers approached me and struck me in my gut, dropping me to the ground. As I laid on the floor, the two men that were with him came over to me and picked me up. Then they followed the first mate to the deck, one carrying me by my arms and the other by my legs.

When we got to the deck, they immediately threw me onto the ground. I assumed at that moment that I was laying on my deathbed. Then I heard Donald's voice (I will no longer address this barbarian as a captain in my diary), and when I adjusted my view towards him, I saw he had a steel-tipped whip in his right hand. Its end was drooling with blood. I then heard a groan, and I immediately noticed someone lying next to his feet on the deck floor with fresh slashes on their back. The person was not an African, but a crewman. And as I looked deeper, I realized it was Charles.

At this revelation, I quickly rose to my feet and demanded to be told what was going on. Donald informed me that Charles had quoted scripture to him about how it was Charles's God-given right to rest on the seventh day, and thus his right to return to his mother's and rest after our next voyage. Then Donald continued by telling me that he did not teach Charles that part of the scripture and that he knew that the other crew members did not teach Charles that as well, so he only had the right to assume that I was the one who had taught Charles.

Before I could even muster a word, Charles arose to his knees and said humbly, with plentiful tears streaming down his face, that it was not I, but rather a friend of his mothers who had taught him scripture and how to read. He stated that was why he wanted to go home, that he wanted to continue his lessons because he had already been under service for two years, and his father had already put in five years of service.

At this, Donald said that he should kill Charles, but quickly retorted himself by saying he owed Charles's father a great debt. Then with the whole crew watching, he told them that this was what happened when they searched scripture alone without his guidance, he their shepherd. That this was what caused the elder Twain's death at sea, the curse that his son had admitted to, Donald then instructed me to take Charles back to my quarters; given that Charles had nursed me while I was ill, I could now return my debt by nursing him. So, at this very moment, Charles lays on my bed in deep anguish. I did not ask about the events that led up to his lashing. I'm forced to remember the atrociousness that occurs on this ship whenever I write in this diary. Therefore, I will not give him that same pain.

Donald also added before me bringing Charles to my quarters that I would also have to take over Charles's duty as the steward. I fear these might be my last words, and if they are, I have instructed Charles to keep my diary and have it brought to my family when the ship ports back in London. I cannot tell you all that I am about to do in this entry, out of fear that someone may come to my quarters and acquire my diary before I do it. But I am taking the information I received from Charles tonight as a sign that I must do what I am about to do. So, to my family, I love you all.

Danial MacAleese
August 11th, 1784

DREAMS

The Classic Edition

August 12th, 1784

I write this entry in great Jubilee. I now know that all things work towards something good. I will begin by telling you of the details I acquired that I was hesitant to share in my last entry, when I was nursing Charles early yesterday morning prior to writing my closing paragraphs to my August 10th entry. I concocted a plan to escape this death ship. I asked Charles if he had given the keys which unlock the slaves to first mate Rogers; he said yes, but that he had told first mate Rogers that Donald wanted Charles to have the keys back right away to return it to him because they were scheduled to speak. So, after first mate Rogers completed the task said to him per the request of Donald, he did just that and returned the keys to him. Charles then followed by informing me that the keys that unlock the slaves from their chains would also open the storeroom. At this, I dropped to my knees and knew what my very purpose of being on this ship.

So, right before sunrise when I knew most of the ship's crew would be hungover in their chambers or outside on the deck floor from their night of wild drinking. I went and collected the slave's provisions to feed them and then free them. I will add that first mate Rogers stopped me in the storage chamber of the ship as I was collecting the food, but I was excused after I told him that I was only doing

Charles's duties. However, before I was able to escape his clutches, he did ask me why I was up so early in the morning, I told him that I had other things to do, he responded by instructing me to step forward. When I did, he grabbed the bucket with the provisions and dumped half of the provisions from the bucket back into the main container where it was stored. He then told me that they did not feed the slaves that much and sent me on my way.

When I got to the hold, I expected to see a lot of the Africans asleep, but many were wide awake. I swiftly then proceeded to hand out the provisions in case first mate Rogers came down to check in on what I was doing. After I believed a couple of minutes had passed by, I made my way to the storeroom. When I reached it, the man with fearless eyes stood up and proceeded to watch me intently as I unlocked its door. I then walked over to the man with fearless eyes and dropped to one knee so that I could unlock the lock on his ankle; I then followed by unlocking his arms and neck.

At this, all the other slave's eyes widened in severe shock, and many started to become restless. Instantly, the man with fearless eyes began to calm them down. I followed this by going into the storeroom and pulling out a sword to which I tossed to the man with fearless eyes. He caught the sword valiantly, and I could tell it was not the first time he had held one.

I then proceeded to unlock the other slaves, and while I would unlock them, the ones who were capable of fighting would go to the storeroom where the man with fearless eyes would hand them a sword. I would say there were about seventy-seven out of the hundred or so that I saw enter the ship on the first day still alive before me in the bunk. Out of those seventy-seven survivors, about forty-five of them were in able fighting shape, and out of those, thirty-seven were able to be armed with blades. We made as little noise as possible amongst each other while all this was happening because we did not want to alarm the crew above us. But we all already knew what was about to happen next.

After everybody was free, the ones that were armed, followed by those who were unarmed, began to make their way to the stairs leading to the upper compartments of the ship. I, too, proceeded to walk with them, trailing only a half-step behind. But as I reached the stairs, the man with fearless eyes stopped me and pointed to where the ones not capable of fighting and children were and nodded to them. I believe it was his way of telling me that this was not my battle.

All we could hear for the next twenty minutes or so were the screams of men and that of steel slashing onto flesh. Though the Africans looked frail because of the conditions they had been confined to, I figured the fight to be fair because they would have the element of surprise because most of the crew would be hungover or still drunk asleep. Additionally, the Africans were fighting for the reason that no darkness can diffuse, freedom.

When it had seemed things were settling down, I quickly made my way back to the deck. All that my eyes saw before me was a massacre of the crew. I assumed all of them to be dead due to how their blood and gore from their hacked bodies painted the ship. I also saw that only a few Africans fell to their doom, but that was still nowhere near the number of the ship's crew. After assessing all I could see on the bottom deck floor, I looked to the top deck, and there stood the man with fearless eyes. He motioned his hand up to which held the head of Donald for all the others to see. He then threw it into the ocean, and the splash from the lifeless head hitting the water was met with shouts of triumph from the Africans. In response, I quickly ran to my quarters to see if Charles was alright. Indeed, the Africans had spared his life.

After quickly relaying the news to Charles of the African's great victory, he told me that he wanted to see all that had unfolded with his own eyes. To his request, I helped him to his feet to show him what the morning's fight for freedom had led to. When we reached the deck, some Africans came and helped us walk to the ship's helm where the man with fearless eyes stood. Upon our arrival to him, he pointed in the opposite direction from which we were sailing; although we could not communicate with words, we understood each other clearly. They wanted to go home. Charles too understood, and so he mustered his strength, grabbed the helm, and managed to turn the ship around with the help of the man with fearless eyes.

I did not do what I did on this day out of bitterness but rather out of morality because it was the right thing to do. I do not know where my journey may take me, but as the Africans, onboard, this ship are sailing back to the coast of Africa to go home, I too pray one day that I shall make it home.

Danial MacAleese
August 12th, 1784

August 16th, 1784

I had thought that I would not be adding
another entry to my diary until we docked
somewhere off the coast of Africa, but due to the
events that occurred today, I felt bewildered if
I did not record them right away. For the past
few days, Charles and I have found ourselves in
excellent communication with the Africans we
were able to help. No way do I say this to give
credit to us both, the Africans fought and won
their battle by slaying the crew. But the
Africans have been keeping a very close watch
intending to all the duties that Charles has
been instructing them to do, to keep us properly
sailing. Some of the Africans went even as far
as to gather some of the plants from the storage
compartment of the ship, to craft up an
ointment to heal the lash marks Donald placed
on Charles. back

How blessed are we that Charles was able to
grab the helm and simultaneously instruct the
Africans so that we have a full crew working to
help us sail. The past days have truly been a
wonder to my eyes, and I surely believe I have
seen the Love of Humanity at work. However,
the road to salvation is not always an easy one.
This morning, as we were continuing to sail
back to the continent of Africa, we saw another
ship sailing in our direction. Everyone
panicked as we all knew what was about to
happen. The ship coming towards us was much

larger than ours. While everyone was in a frenzy, the man with fearless eyes took charge of the situation once again. He instructed the children and those not able to fight to get to the lower compartments of the ship, along with Charles and myself. I refuted his order, for I wished to show my courage, but he nodded toward the children as they were descending to the chambers. I fully understood the task that had bestowed upon me, and I readily accepted.

For the next thirty minutes, the ship was consumed with the sounds of gunfire, swords slashing onto human flesh, and the haunting echo of the screams of men falling to their death. All the children held each other tightly as the battle raged over us. When a few minutes of things settling down had passed, we heard footsteps descending to where we were. I thanked God that it was the man with fearless eyes who walked into the room; we all breathed a deep sigh of relief at his sight, and all the children began to sing and dance in joy.

We quickly followed him up the stairs, and upon reaching the deck, we saw the other ship, three times the size of our own, directly to the side of ours. Many slaves from the other ship had made it to their deck, and the two ships were connected so that everybody could move freely back and forth between the vessels by way of planks to which looked as if they were dropped on our ship by the other during its failed attempted raid. I saw many Africans on the deck of the other ship; I believe there had to be at least eighty of them, and that's not counting the ones still in the lower compartments.

As I observed all that was before my eyes, one of the Africans from the other ship quickly rushed at me with a drawn sword. Out of nowhere came the man with fearless eyes, who deflected my attacker's blow with his sword. If he had not done this, my attacker's sword would have fatally pierced me, for it was poised for my chest. When my attacker attempted another lunge at me, he was countered by a kick to his face, by the man with fearless eyes. At this, more Africans from the other ship, attempted to quickly rush in on both me and Charles, who was standing at my side. However, the man with fearless eyes stepped in front of us and held his arms out, as if to shield us. The men who were charging at us stopped at this gesture, and then scornfully looked at Charles and me. Then the man with fearless eyes began to deliberate with them, to which he was joined by other men and women from our ship. How odd I thought life was at this moment, the men and women we had once been shipping to their doom, were now defending us from our own. I now know to take nothing for granted; every day I live, I have been seeing Loves blessings being bestowed upon me.

After a few hours had passed, everyone that was initially aboard the ship Judah moved to the newer and bigger vessel, to which has more food, room, and will make for a faster time sailing. We're right now in the process of turning this ship around, by the leadership of Charles, to return to the continent of Africa. Granted, I do not know where my journey will take me, but I gladly leave it in the hands of fate.

Danial MacAleese
August 16th, 1784

August 29th, 1784

After nearly two weeks of sailing the vessel we came to acquire, we have finally reached a beach coast on the vast continent of Africa. Although we're all not quite sure where we are, I genuinely believe we're with good company, which is the hand of fate. These last weeks aboard this ship have been truly wondrous.

The Africans are not much different from us; everything that Donald told me was a lie. I knew such was the case when he spoke it, but I would often wonder whether he knew he was speaking lies or if he believed what he was saying. Because if anybody took a minute out of their lives to interact with these people, they would see they are just like us and not the savages, we're often led to believe that they are. I am ashamed that I ever agreed to be an overseer to them, but I am glad that I have been given salvation through my shortcomings.

I am afraid, though, that this will be my last entry in this diary. I know I promised to write about my adventures in America, but fate had a more excellent plan for me. I do wish, however, that one day I will be able to return home to Belfast. Granted, I am not sure how it will happen, but as I stated before, I leave everything to fate.

Charles says he will continue to walk north along the coast until he reaches a port, but I have decided to go into the jungle with the

Africans. I'll be leaving my diary in Charles's hands, as he has promised me that he would figure out a way to have it delivered to my family in Belfast. I ask you not to think ill of me for not returning to you all right away, but something is calling to my heart, creating a burden that I must fulfill. I am sorry if all this seems so short and out of nowhere. The time I spent with the Africans on this journey has meant a lot to me. I feel that there is much more for me to learn from them.

Danial MacAleese
August 29th, 1784

ACT 6:

THE PATH

TO

LOVE

Poetic Justice

Running on Love, go ahead and check my transmission

Seen my mama struggle, so nothing can stop me

From the jungle, so I'm always ready for the rumble

Just became the World's Greatest

Quote the veins cold; I'm not one for the fumbles

Shots wet even when there's pressure.

Don't mistake the boast It's All Love

I'm coming with it humble

Finally got the keys to my locks

Now will see who they'll be calling Dumbo

It's crazy how bad they want to see us crumble

Good thing I got Dreams of hollering out to my Sisters'

Jambo!

A Dreamers Expiration

They say a Dream is what you make of it

I just pray that your Heart Dreamt of it

And Love is what projects it

Because the world has a funny way of interpreting it

Testifying riches should be what comes of it

But what good is the world

If you lose your soul in return?

Can't take sixty million with you when you're deceased.

The Classic Edition

Windows To My Soul

Tell me what do you see when you look into my eyes?

Do you see pain?

Do you see pride?

Do you see the Love from the pleasures of my lust?

Do you see a sinner lost in a sea of his guilt?

Frantically panicking trying to swim back to shore

Because the life he lives, he can no longer harbor?

University Ave (Dirty Dinky)

They tell me I'll never fit the mold I swear sometimes this world is too cold

I'm just trying to share a story of a young man on a quest for a Golden paved road

That's a road to dreams that can't even be imagined when you sleep

I swear they hate it when we're deep

They would rather have us talking about who's next to us when we sleep

You know the saying' If your body count ain't in the double digits boy you're weak?

That's the reason we stroll through University Ave at night the end of each week

You know hoping to find a live party with a couple thick freaks

Don't judge me we're all off that drink

That's fireball and some gin

That's why their cinnamon kisses taste like sin

But we never care because we live in a generation where the motto is' If we score we win

They tell me I'll never fit the mold I swear sometimes this world is too cold

I'm just trying to share a story of a young man on a quest for a Golden paved road

That's a road to dreams that can't even be imagined when you sleep

I swear they hate it when we're deep

They would rather have our minds asleep

The Classic Edition

Greatness

Whomsoever shall be great amongst you

Shall be your servant

Wise words from a Friend

On a matter of great importance

Cause selfishness can leave a world divided

So, Greatness He redefined it

By Love, the only thing to which can unite US

The Keys To Greatness

Humble yourselves

Before Love becomes a blur to you

That means being merciful to others while in your endeavors

Can you tell me what's the fare to your sinful affairs?

See mercy only causes us to grow a few gray hairs

That's wisdom if you didn't know

So, know it's better to be last than first

It's more glorious to be called to the front from the back

Then to be sent to the back from the front

Sometimes the truth doesn't need to rhyme

The Classic Edition

The Blessings Of Greatness

Always be thankful for your tribulations

Love can never be conquered

See different trials will bless you with different results

I'm talking of changes

That can't be found inside your couch

Just believe, and you shall receive

You can only see the Stars upon a night sky

So, allow the hard times to illuminate your Heart

Hidden Treasures

What if living out your Dreams was as easy as falling asleep?

Would it even last because it's easily achieved?

Just some food for thought to nourish your soul

With hopes that it aids you in your growth

So, this is written for kids hearing more gunshots than sirens

Kids seeing more crack heads than fathers

Teachers trying to make us a little bit smarter

Falsely believing degrees is the only way will get to our Master

This is written for those of us facing bad weather

Wondering if they were pressured in error

Not knowing through pressure comes treasure

The Classic Edition

All Eyes On Me (The Last Stretch)

Back like I never felt
Hungrier than I've ever been
Now we run the map
Finally got my Heart on track
Call this the Victory lap
Fighting like I'm on my last
Call this the Final stretch
I said words fire it'll ignite a match
Thank God, my blessings don hatch
Now world domination is what follows next
I said' If all the worlds a stage then I'm on deck
King can't kill my thunder
This is Simba when he came to get his kingdom back
These words are just my roar
I pray Love is here is the message absorbed
You can prey but will never greet defeat
Peep, this vision too deep
Couldn't even Dream it up in your sleep
Look mama,
I got all the kids reading what you mean to me

Me Against The World Part 5 (So Many Tears)

It's been hard for me to smile lately, can't front I've been wanting to die lately, been waiting for my blessings to fall, but each day I awake with my back still up against the wall

If there's a God watching over me, you know I've been given it my all

So why do you remain on stall? Can't you see life's trying me?

Fear of my Mama getting a heart attack, the only thing prolonging this tragedy

Pardon my suicidal mentality, but I 'm not a Christian, I'm not perfect

The liquor and drugs only thing prolonging this tragedy

Heard broken pieces are supposed to reveal the light in you, but all my Heart's spilling is these tears that I'm leaking, I'm scared to die, but I haven't been doing much living

Pardon my suicidal mentality, but if there's a God watching over me, can you tell me what is it that you want from me?

They say patience is key

But why should I have to suffer for inner peace? Shouldn't the end exist within the means?

The Classic Edition

Keep Your Head Up (Loves Mentality)

Is there still no hope for the future?

I just heard an 11-year-old in my bible study class say he wants to be a preacher

I swear those words touched my soul

Cause when I look into his eyes I see a future great leader

I thank his mother for the way he was brought up in this cold world

See she be working doubles, but she still finds a way to show him he's her world

And that's what I see in his eyes the drive to give her the world

You know take her from riding buses to rides from chauffer's

Show her he wouldn't be anything if it wasn't all for her

(Break)

Is there still no hope for the future?

My homies got babies, and they're planning to stay for their futures

My Brother Robert gave up an out of state football scholarship just to be there the first time his son smiled

Now every time I ask him of his son he smiles

He once told me of how he's going to raise him to be a better man than he was because he didn't have a father to warn him of the trials of life

I told him'
If your son is half the man you are then he's going to
be great

You're actually here bro, so your actions will speak
louder than any speech you ever give him

You're a hero, a nineteen-year-old father who didn't
run from the pressure but walked to it only to discover
it was your treasure

(Break)

Is there still no hope for the future?

I know this Sister that got mad dreams for her future

Glenridge kid if you met her you wouldn't even think
her parents were users

She once told me she wants to be a tutor

For kids that the world says have no future

You know the ones that aspire to be pushers and
shooters

The ones that didn't make the cut to meet college
recruiters

I asked her one day though'
What makes you think they are going to listen to you?

She replied back with'
How do you know someone really Loves you?

(Break)

The Classic Edition

Is there still no hope for the future?

My Brother Dimitri used to tell me when he died he was sure he would see hell

See he was just a lost child in a cold world who saw sin as the only thing that sells

Plus, it didn't help that when he would turn on televisions screens

He saw that's the only way that people that looked like him excelled

And he didn't have A pops, so statistics would tell him that his destination was a cell

He asked me once'
What is a brother to do? I don't have anything to lose, but I can't help but feel blue, I want to talk to God so bad, but it's been a minute, and I'm scared he might not recognize my voice cause of all this pain I've let build up inside my Heart so will you pray for me? cause I feel death waiting on me

I said back to him'
Always know from Gods heart you'll never depart

Every path has a start

Yeah, my Brother, I'll pray for you

But only you can control your restart.

DREAMS

The Classic Edition

ACT 7:

THE JOYS

OF

LOVE

DREAMS

The Classic Edition

Love Yours (I Believe I Can Fly)

Tell me, how should I flow?

Should I give you grace, or speak about race?

Maybe this intro was a mistake

But if I were to erase

I wouldn't be showing you my true face

So, if I said it, then I mean it

This is a story of a born sinner turned winner

Please tell me if you've seen it! Words notorious

Flow Michael Jackson when he wrote off the wall

Got the world as my stage

But I'm trying to walk on the moon

See if you shoot for the stars

You'll have nothing to lose

These words are how I broke loose from my noose

The chains of slavery are now bound to our minds

So, I pray these words you consume

The enemy is who you see in the mirror

And I pray you'll call truce

Your soul is all that you got to lose

And that can't ever be reproduced

Redemptions Poem

If you look back at your past

How can you move forward to your future?

Life isn't an easy road

But listen closely'

To receive your award

You must first free your soul

Your mind is only what you know

Your Heart is the path you'll go

The Classic Edition

Real Change

From the Go like Simba

This the Hakuna Matata way

So, it's in the name of Love, like Timon would say

But before Nala returns to me today

Can I at least get the right words to say?

I know Love never strays, but it's been a while

I hope this time she chills and stays awhile

I know now it's not about you being mine

But rather you being with me

Not as an idol but as a part of me

Oh, how I miss watching you cheese ever so silly

Homecoming (Chaining Day)

My only DREAM now

Is when I kneel to My God

He says to me'

My Son, a Job Well done

Don't need the world to Praise me

For where I've come from

My story is His Glory

I pray you feel the songs I've sung

Even though my work is so small

Truth be told, meaningless in all

But still, I pray that when I kneel in front of My God

With tears of joy strolling down my face

As the Angels of Heaven Praise His name

He says to me'

My Son, a Job Well Done.

The Classic Edition

Better Days (The World's Greatest)

Just got up out of the valley of the shadow of death

Mama, your baby boy, finally free at last

Got a new game plan to leave all my troubles in the past

Casted all my lots

So, I won't even look back

Whoever thought a pawn would access the manifest to be King

The key was I had to learn how to adapt

Wasn't easy though

Took some punches along the path

But I was born hungry

So, like bowls those blows I ate

This is the prayer from the wilderness

That just got served

Now observe as I win my enemies over

On like every verse

Me Against The World Part 6 (Let God Down)

If this is my last verse

Then know I didn't do it for God

But rather the kids that look like me

I'm talking of the kids that Dreamed like me

The ones that came from nothing

But in a smile, they still believed

Yeah, that's who I tried to reach

Paint to them that there is no peak

Yeah, the sky's the limit

But only as far as their arms can reach

So, this is to the ones on their tippy-toes

Cause Love you can't teach

I'm talking of the fatherless and godless

Cause we born underprivileged

See cause a real creator would protect us

What pride does one have that it takes a dying man having to beg you for help for you to save him?

It's funny how God wants us to hail Him

But the only thing preventing this suicide is the heartbreak of our Mothers feeling they failed us

The Classic Edition

(Extended Remix)

Lately, it's been hard for me not to smile

Cause all I can see is freedom in my sights

See I'm no longer afraid to die

Because it will be the day I return home

To the land where my Heart Resides.

THE END

BUT REALLY, IT'S JUST
THE NEW BEGINNING

Tonight's The Night (World Tour)
Coming Soon To A City Near You!!!

DREAMS

The Classic Edition

DREAMS

The Classic Edition

I don't wanna die no more
The storm is over
And I don't wanna cry no more
But I can't help but weep tears of joy
See I think I made it
I'm always smiling, and Love is the reason

I'm trying to preserver like tomorrow doesn't exist

They say always save the best for last

While I guess I'll persist

I'm just trying to give you my prerequisite

But don't trip I'm no valedictorian

Cause to be honest I barely made it

But you know what they say'

When the Praises go up, The Blessings come down

Graduated from a pawn to a King

And Love was the Key

My bad if I'm preaching in circles

I'm just trying to let you know this well is deep

Never knew this cooling water would taste so sweet

This is the Victory Lap

That's why I entitled this psalm grab your Dreams

This that reach for the stars

So, if you fall you land on a cloud

And if you do brush yourself off and go for it again

You know you're Heaven sent

When your hunger never ends

Text messages' Congratulations I seen you made it

Replied back' We're just getting started

The Classic Edition

I don't wanna die no more
The storm is over
And I don't wanna cry no more
But I can't help but weep tears of joy
See I think I made it
I'm always smiling, and Love is the reason

They say a frown can turn the whole world upside down
So, allow me to prescribe to you a few words
For if ever you're feeling down
As you walk on this road called life
Know gray clouds doesn't last forever
I mean even in the darkest night
Why do you think the moon is shining for?
Faith is knowing the hard road your walking on
Will one day turn Gold
Nothing good comes easy
But nothing is more beautiful than a Dream achieved
If Love inspired your vision
Then know by Love's grace you shall achieve
Never lose Hope, Always Believe
That means when trouble comes just say' Cheese

(DREAMS)
I'm not here to sell you DREAMS
See inspirations are free
I'm just doing this for the kids that have nothing to believe
Can you please tell me what is there for us to achieve
When reaching 21 means, you overachieved?
Thought having a black president was meant to be our relieve
But whenever I turn on the T.V.
I see another Brother deceased
But all Brothers seem to care about
Are when the new Jordan's getting released

The Classic Edition

Every day isn't perfect
But that doesn't mean it doesn't have a purpose
Yes, happiness comes and goes
But know Joy they can't ever take that from you
Please don't ever forget
A frown will bring the whole world down
When you smile it's a reflection of how your soul shines
Don't you know that darkness will never conquer light?
Remember that's why stars shine the brightest at night
Rainy seasons don't last forever
So, when it feels like December
Always remember September
April showers are just Blessings descending
Why else do you think May brings flowers?

(DREAMS)
Pardon me I don't always try to reach
But they'll always critique you when your messages deep
Especially when the kids are who you try to reach
They fear us when Love is what we seek
That's why they blind us with stresses that deceive
But what happens when keeping it real goes bad?
To it, I ask' Can you buy your soul back?
That's a parable for the ones
Who know life is about We
That's a wakeup call for the ones
Who think everything is about me

The Classic Edition

If thou have run with the footman
And they have worried thee
Then how can thou contend with horses?
Peep unprovoked trouble
Just means your finish line is approaching
Why else do you think it snows on top of mountains?
Got DREAMS to see the fountain of youth
Heard a sip of its Waters can dry all your tears away

(DREAMS)
Who speaks to the voiceless?
Cause I see the youth looking hopeless
Their hearts are fragile like lotus
So, what's with this hocus pocus
In trying to hoax us?
Cause trapping leaves us Roadless
And rapping leaves us Soulless
Is our death your bonus!?
Pardon my boldness
But I just can't help but feel the coldness
It's cool though
Cause see I got DREAMS that one day
All the kids gonna quote this
"Till I'm in Heaven, I'm homeless."
The Classic Edition

For Our Eyes Only (The Storm Is Over Now)

If these are my last words

Let it be my exhale

I've seen the top of the mountain

The system wasn't meant for us to excel

These words are just the harvest of a mustard seed

See I'm just trying to live out my DREAMS

Love with me so best believe I'll succeed

Each line is how I flap my wings

I'm not gloating who says we can't all win?

But know it's hard to see the sun under stress cliffs

But back to the topic

Why else do you think caged birds sing?

Praise is the key it'll set you free

That's a warning

So, beware of the lyrics you recite faithfully

I'm talking of the ones that entice you to live dangerously

In this world, we've been Blessed, to know what Love is

So, who says we can't all win big?

This is the moment of truth

What type of soil are you?

Remember, real change resides only in you.

The Classic Edition

CREDITS

Thank You to Kendall Witaszek, for the hours spent editing this book surely this couldn't have been done without You, You ma'am are what I like to call a Blessing.

Thank You to Yyonger Wilson, for giving me a template for this book and always being a Loving listener of my craziness, If You weren't there for me, in the beginning, to encourage me I don't think I would have taken this book as serious as I did I can't say Thank You enough.

Thank You to Dimitra Kaulu, I will forever remember the night you told me to stay true to my Heart when I write, by never forgetting where I come from. That seed You planted forever changed the course of my writings. Also, Thank You for always being You, everything that I try to do is an artistic inspiration of You, Forever and Always my Da Vinci.

I can Thank so many more people, but if I named everybody, it would have to be its own book. So, to everyone who has influenced me by their Love, Thank You, it takes a Village to Raise a Child.

BLESSINGS (VICTORY OVER FEAR)

My intuition is telling me your Blessings are here
Just hold out your hand and receive
Good things come to those who prayed
You know the enemy has a lot to say
When you're shinning at the top
But that's why Light cast's out shade
Remember to whom can A Lion be prey!
Stand tall and be brave
Declare all your troubles Love will take
And say it with your chest
So, the world knows We don't play
Rise of the DREAMERS
Our era of reign is here to stay
Oh, Happy Day

The Classic Edition

DREAMS

The Classic Edition

205

DREAMS

The Classic Edition

www.ingramcontent.com/pod-product-compliance
Lightning Source LLC
LaVergne TN
LVHW011347080426
835511LV00005B/178